This is a work of personal thoughts. Unless otherwise indicated, all the names, characters, businesses, places, events and incidents in this book are the product of the author's, personal experience, imagination, or used in a fictitious manner. Any resemblance to actual persons, living or dead, or actual events is purely coincidental. So, chill.

Natalie Bassie

What We'te Working With

(Or The Trial and Tribulation of Making Sense of Your Early 20s)

For Blake
and Emily
and for seeing what was always
within

Cover photo by Lainey Kineer

I wrote because I could not make sense all of the things floating in my head.

You can be anything

You don't get to see
The whereabouts
Of me
Who I've become
Since then
And who
I will continue to be

You don't get to see
The boys I've met and
The places I've wept
Who held my hand
And where I now
Buy bread -

You don't get to see
The weight I've gained
Since you left my space
Oh! How you took up my space!
Only for the sake
Of wanting to feel seemingly free

Pho the love

Our Pho was hot that day
Like the sun warming up
The grass with its rays
In late May

She whispered to me,
"Girl, you look small."

"So? I have always been."

The scale claimed the name
One above eighty-eight
I could tell I was
Shrinking just to dissipate

A comical thing
To allow yourself to recoil
To then have your body then
Follow down the street
That taking up less space
Is the way to
Stay in another's race.

Back for two, I leave in June

I always cry when I get back home
Not because I miss home
Just because when I am home I am alone

I'm in every group message imaginable
Yet there is a still a void so undeniable

And you'll say to me,
"Oh, God can fix that!"
And I will say back,
"Is this how to dismiss
Someone under 5'6"?"

But I know
I will find
Him

Not in your cliches
You've heard since you
Were eight

But in the quiet places
When night falls
And lamenting is the only song
I find that pulls me in
To find a place to rest

                    The house on the avenue
The familiarity of front porch steps
With that one creak on the third floor

And the front door
Always unlocked
Up until eleven o'clock

With the piano in the back room
And the coolness that enters
The tiny family room

They say
"If walls could speak, they'd have a lot to say!"

But I think they slept all day
And we are the ones
That have much more to say

About our time on the front porch
With that one creak on the third floor
And the man on his bike
That peddles by
Before midnight

Will you kiss me goodnight?

I don't know, you tell me.
We are only 21, 22, 23,
Yet we think we know about
As much as
My Grandpa

He would have been
93 in the spring

The truth of the matter is
We are all
Scared
Frail
Unprepared

Trying to project to
Those around
That we are
Flawless
Honest
Cautious

But i wonder
If it's much more honest
To harness a sense
Of heart felt
Awareness

That none of us know what we're talking about.

23 in 2023

Maybe I am
Falling
In

Like
-or-

Maybe I am
Dreaming about
Playing piano
With you
In your house's back den

While your tall friends scream
Downstairs because
They found
The movie to be too rude

What will life be like
At 23?

Will it be with you?
Now, hold my hand before
The sky turns blue

Shake

I am sorry you
Blamed me for
Your voicelessness

Taking up space
Is a brave thing to be

Perhaps something
Unfamiliar
To your being?

When it is easier
To stick to something
Not new.

Something that feels
Familiar and not
Out of the blue

Oh, what a wasted life
To play it
cool.

Tell me

On the off chance that my soul should forget, tell me again:

That you are aware of my fragile soul
That you still
Have it
In full control

To know that you are for me
Even in the mundane
And things unseen

To know that you still see me
Even when I do not care to see you

To know that I am
Loved
Even when I surrender to shame

Tell me to fall back to you.

Evangelical

But they had
A verse in their
Insta bio

I saw

But they seem to only show
Great faith on
The Lord's Day of Sundays

Is faith a two-way street?

Where I am known to be a follower
Of a Man who entered into a city
On Palm Sunday

Where the Potter has His way
Every hour of the day

Where His love is more radiant than a midsummer's ray
Where I am called to love
Those who others find to be
Ugly runaways

Including the runaways who are
Only up to love
On Sundays

No more

Its not my favorite
Place anymore

No longer a street
I would call home

Just a place with
Lots of rooms
With a decent view

One in which
I am happy I outgrew

I know the backway
Past the after church crowd
To get back

But the last time
I did that
My friend witnessed
A panic attack
At the traffic light
Next to the new chain
Restaurant

I am not
Who I was
Those
Four years
Ago

And I hope
As the seasons
Change
I long for this
Soul to continue to rearrange
And work through the pain
That seems to
Upstage the
Growth gained -

And we are safe

Thank God
It never came to be
That being what
I thought I wanted it
To be

But it turned into
Opposite
Of what I thought I needed

Truly
Who would want sleepless nights of tear
Stained pillows
And walking around on eggshells all
Throughout the month of December?

Never knowing what the tide would bring
But pondering, will I live in this constant state
Of fear and sorrow?

Sarasota, Florida in the Spring

50 States
Could never contain
The ache
Of being without you

And the plane lands
In a hometown
I wish I wasn't so acquainted with

And heres comes
The come down
With barely
Touching the omelets
My dad makes for me
The next two days

Staring at the floorboards
And wishing for the phone to ring
Sooner than our
Designated
Late night phone dates

I adore a soul
Who is states away
But is my real home

Enemies and friends

You can't hurt me
Because I won't let you

Make me feel small
And treat me
As a foreigner

Underneath it all
You are scared
We all are too

How much longer
Until you too
Run away from
You?

You can't hurt me
Because I won't let you

Treat me again
Like anything
Like anyone

Because I don't know you
And I no longer
Let you know me

Who was me?

I got water
Because you always ragged on soda

And I got vegetables
Because the sugar was never up to par

I lost myself
Trying to find the version
That you insisted
You wanted

Is this the version you?
Disconnected and dishonest?

1 Kings

Maybe I need more sleep?

But maybe there is more underneath.

That needs to be seen

And sorted out

And cleaned.

Maybe I need more sleep?

But maybe there is a tear stained pillow

I still find that makes out your name

From the terrors of the night

That you have somehow marked since June

Maybe I need more sleep?

Or maybe I'm just weak

And somehow I'm suppose to boast

About that

And what about that?

Maybe the weakness

Is where I somehow find

The nearness of

You.

Maybe I need more sleep?

To wake up

To find

You were there

Holding me through the night.

Time and time and time

Some things
Are just too coincidental
A year
For example
I was the fool
Running
And loosing
You were true

Some things
Are just too coincidental
A year
For example
Tornadoes and storms
Dances and grins
And me being the fool

Some things
Are just too coincidental
A year
For example
Me staying true
But you acting
As if
You are someone no one
Ever truly true

And spring is here
With her need to bloom
I must go too